1 *Crypto for Beginners*

Copyright ©**James B. Solis**

All relevant Reserved

This book's content cannot be reproduced, stored, or transmitted in any form without the copyright owner's permission. This includes electronic or mechanical means, photocopying, recording, or any other method.

Table of Contents

- About the book
-
- INTRODUCTION

- CHAPTER 1

- Essential Information to Begin Investing.
- Risk and Return:
- Investment Accounts:
- How to Master Crypto Even if You're a Total Novice.
- Crucial Information You Need to Know Before Trading Crypto
- How to Profit from Cryptocurrency Always.
- How to Prevent Cryptocurrency Scams.
- Be Wary of Scams and
- Phishing:

- → CHAPTER 2
- → Types of Cryptocurrencies
- → Bitcoin: The Pioneer
- → Impact on the Crypto World:
- → New Cryptocurrencies to Watch
- → The Significance of Emerging Cryptocurrencies:

- ★ CHAPTER 3
- ★ Configuring an Online Portfolio
- ★ Depositories versus Non-Depositories:
- ★ Selecting a Crypto Exchange.
- ★ Purchasing Your First Bit of Bit Coin
- ★ Purchasing Your First Bit of Bit Coin

- CHAPTER 4
- Comprehending Blockchain Technology.
- Fundamentals of Blockchain.
- Proof of Work (PoW):
- Proof of Stake (PoS):
- Decentralized Applications (DApps)

- CHAPTER 5
- Buying, Selling, and Trading Cryptocurrency.
- How to Trade Cryptocurrencies 101
- Principles Crucial to Trading: -
- Market Demand and Supply:
- Day trading versus long-term investing.

- ☐ CHAPTER 6
- ☐ Mining Cryptocurrencies
- ☐ What is Mining Crypto?
- ☐ How Mining Operates:
- ☐ Evidence of Stake vs. Proof of Work
- ☐ What Is Superior?
- ☐ Application-Specific Integrated Circuits (ASICs):

- ★ CHAPTER 7
- ★ Privacy and Security with Cryptocurrency
- ★ Phishing scams: (1)
- ★ How to Avoid:
- ★ Idle Coin Offerings, or Fake ICOs:

CHAPTER 8
- ❖ Global Regulations Regarding Cryptocurrencies
- ❖ New Advancements:
- ❖ Determining Gains:

CHAPTER 9

- The future of virtual currencies.
- Blockchain Interoperability Development:
- Cryptocurrency's Place in the World
- Investing and Conjecturing:
- Opportunity:
- Environmental Impact and Scalability:
- DeFi and Web3 Evolution:
-

Crypto for Beginners and All

About the book

Crypto for Beginners and All is a comprehensive guide designed to demystify the world of cryptocurrencies for both newcomers and seasoned enthusiasts.
 The book walks readers through the essentials of cryptocurrency, offering clear explanations of key concepts like blockchain technology, crypto trading, and digital wallets.
It is crafted to help anyone, regardless of their prior knowledge, understand how cryptocurrencies like Bitcoin, Ethereum, and others operate in today's digital economy.

Starting with the basics,
Crypto for Beginners and All delves into the history and evolution of digital currencies, giving readers a solid foundation in the space. The book further explains how to safely invest, trade, and store crypto, ensuring that readers are

equipped with the knowledge to manage risks and avoid scams. It explores key topics such as decentralized finance (DeFi), crypto mining, and the regulatory environment that shapes the industry.

For those looking to profit or simply learn more about the future of finance, this guide serves as a practical roadmap. With real-world examples and easy-to-understand language,

Crypto for Beginners and All is a must-read for anyone looking to confidently step into the dynamic world of cryptocurrency.

James B. Solis

INTRODUCTION

Cryptocurrency For Beginners in particular, the world of cryptocurrencies might appear confusing and perplexing. But at its foundation, a cryptocurrency is just a type of virtual or digital money that is secured by encryption. You will learn the fundamentals of cryptocurrency in this introduction, including what it is, how it was created, how it operates, and the underlying technology that makes it possible.

How does cryptocurrency work? A digital asset intended to be used as a medium of trade is cryptocurrency. Cryptocurrencies are decentralized, which means they are not issued or managed by a central authority like a government or bank, in contrast to conventional currencies like the dollar or naira. Rather, they function through a technology known as blockchain, which guarantees immutability, security, and transparency. **Key Features:** - Decentralization: The network is not governed by a single body.

Peer-to-Peer Transactions: Direct transactions between parties are possible with cryptocurrencies, negating the need for middlemen.

Security: Cryptography regulates the generation of new units and secures transactions.

Global Accessibility: Participation is open to anybody with an internet connection. While they can be used to purchase goods and services, the use of cryptocurrencies is still restricted when compared to regular currencies. They are frequently kept in digital wallets. The original and most well-known cryptocurrency, Bitcoin, was developed as a substitute for the established financial system.

Cryptocurrency History.

Digital currency is not a brand-new idea. Its origins can be found in the 1980s and 1990s, when initiatives were made to develop digital currency. However, the lack of adoption and technical constraints caused these early initiatives to fail.

The Bitcoin Origin Story: The true innovation happened in 2008 when a whitepaper named "Bitcoin: A Peer-to-Peer Electronic Cash System" was published by an unidentified individual or group of individuals going by the pseudonym Satoshi Nakamoto. In this paper, the decentralized digital currency known as Bitcoin—which runs on a peer-to-peer network and lets users send and receive money without depending on a central authority—was launched. In January 2009, Nakamoto mined the first block, referred to as the "genesis block," which marked the formal beginning of Bitcoin. The Bitcoin age began with this occasion.

The History of the Cryptocurrency Market:
 Initial Growth: Libertarians and computer enthusiasts began to take an interest in Bitcoin. As of 2010, its user and development community was small but increasing.
Introduction of Altcoins: Other cryptocurrencies, referred to as altcoins, started to surface as Bitcoin's appeal increased.

Examples are Ethereum (2015), which introduced the idea of smart contracts, and Litecoin (2011), which was intended to be a "lighter" version of Bitcoin. -

Market Expansion: In 2017, an influx of new initiatives and Initial Coin Offerings (ICOs) propelled the cryptocurrency market's phenomenal rise. When the price of Bitcoin skyrocketed, cryptocurrencies gained widespread attention.

Regulatory Scrutiny and Adoption: As a result of governments and financial institutions becoming more aware of cryptocurrencies, a variety of regulatory measures as well as increasing adoption across a range of industries resulted.

How Digital Assets Operate Cryptography, decentralized networks, and blockchain technology are the fundamental components of cryptocurrency.

Here is a condensed description of the steps involved:

Blockchain Technology: All cryptocurrency transactions are recorded in a public digital ledger called the blockchain. This ledger is decentralized, which means that multiple computers, or nodes, maintain it as opposed to a single central authority.

Every transaction is collected into a "block," which is subsequently appended to a series of preceding blocks to form an unbroken and uninterrupted transaction history. 2

. **Cryptographic Security**: A key component of network security is cryptography. Every transaction is signed and encrypted with a private key that is exclusive to each user. In addition to ensuring that only the cryptocurrency's owner may start a transaction, this guards against fraud and illegal access.

Mechanisms of Decentralization and Consensus:

Coins such as Proof of Work (PoW) and Proof of Stake (PoS) use consensus procedures to make sure the network runs without a central authority. By using these techniques, the network may reach consensus regarding the legitimacy of transactions and preserve the blockchain's integrity.

Proof of Work (PoW): To validate transactions and add them to the blockchain, miners compete by working through challenging mathematical puzzles. Significant computational power and energy are needed for this process. **Proof of Stake (PoS)**: Under PoS, the quantity of coins that validators are willing to "stake" as collateral determines whether or not they are selected to create new blocks.

PoW is not as energy-efficient as this strategy.

Wallets and Keys: Users require a digital wallet to communicate with cryptocurrency networks. This wallet houses their public and private keys. The private key functions similarly to a password that you use to access your funds and sign transactions, but the public key functions as an account number that lets people transfer you cryptocurrency. **Transactions**: A user must make a transaction in their wallet, sign it with their private key, and broadcast it to the network in order to transmit cryptocurrency to another user. The transfer is then finalized when the network validates the transaction and adds it to the blockchain.

Contents for Blockchain Technology.
The underlying technology that drives cryptocurrency is called blockchain. All transactions are recorded using a distributed, decentralized ledger that is accessible to all computers on the network.

Here is a closer look at its operation:
A Blockchain's Structure: A list of transactions is contained in each block that makes up a blockchain.

By joining these pieces chronologically, a chain is created.
Every block has a special identification known as a "hash," which is generated from the block's contents. To guarantee that all blocks are securely connected, the hash of each block also includes the hash of the one before it.

Transparency and Immutability: It is very difficult to change or remove data from a block once it has been put to the blockchain.

A crucial component of blockchain technology is its immutability, which guarantees the confidentiality and integrity of the data. Furthermore, the complete transaction history is visible and verifiable because anyone may access the blockchain, which is open to the public.

Decentralization: A blockchain is kept up to date by a network of nodes, as opposed to conventional databases that are managed by a single entity. Every node takes part in the validation of fresh transactions and possesses a copy of the blockchain. Because it is decentralized, there is no longer a need for middlemen, and the possibility of single points of failure is decreased.

Smart Contracts and DApps: Blockchain technology not only facilitates transaction processing but also the development of smart contracts, which are self-executing contracts that have the conditions of the agreement encoded directly into the code. Without the need for middlemen, these contracts immediately come into effect when the requirements are satisfied. Smart contracts are utilized by decentralized applications (DApps) to offer a range of services, including gaming and finance, and they are developed on blockchain platforms like Ethereum. **Uses Not Limited to Cryptocurrency**: Blockchain has several potential uses outside of cryptocurrencies, even if that's how it's most usually linked with them. Blockchain is being investigated by a number of industries, including finance, real estate, healthcare, and supply chain management, to increase security, efficiency, and transparency.

CHAPTER 1

Essential Information to Begin Investing.

Gaining an understanding of the fundamentals of investing:
Asset Classes: Become acquainted with the different asset classes, such as stocks, bonds, real estate, mutual funds, exchange-traded funds, and cryptocurrencies.

Risk and Return:

Gain knowledge of how risk and possible rewards are related. Risks are typically higher when returns are higher. -
Diversification: To lower risk, distribute assets among several asset classes.

Time Horizon: Establish your investment time horizon to inform your strategy and asset allocation. - **Compound Interest**: Recognize the advantages of long-term investing by understanding how compound interest operates.

Investment Accounts:

- Types: Acquire knowledge about various investment accounts, such as taxable brokerage accounts, retirement accounts (401(k), and individual savings accounts). **Implications for Taxes:** Recognize the tax ramifications of various account kinds and investment gains.

Research and Analysis: - Investment Research: Assess potential investments using analytical tools, market reports, and financial news.

Due Diligence: Investigate prospective investments in-depth to learn about their track record, associated dangers, and current state of the market.

How to Master Crypto Even if You're a Total Novice.

Become Informed: - Basic Ideas: Begin by understanding the basic ideas behind blockchain technology, cryptocurrencies, and how they operate. **Resources**: To lay a solid basis, make use of books, credible websites, and online courses.

Keep Up to Date: - News and Trends: Monitor reputable sources for news, updates, and market trends related to cryptocurrencies.

Groups: Participate in online forums and groups to talk with other professionals and enthusiasts. .

Practical Experience: - Start Small: To obtain real-world experience without taking on large financial risks, start with modest investments. **Test**: Try out various trading methods and tools with demo accounts or tiny stakes.

Gain Knowledge from Professionals: **Podcasts and Webinars**: To obtain deeper understanding and advanced information, tune in to podcasts and webinars presented by cryptocurrency professionals.

Readings and Writings: Examine books and articles authored by knowledgeable cryptocurrency analysts and investors.

Crucial Information You Need to Know Before Trading Crypto

Market Volatility:
Volatility: The price volatility of cryptocurrencies is well-known.
Be ready for large fluctuations in price. - **Control of Risk:** Put risk management techniques into practice, such as placing stop-loss orders and only making investments you can afford to lose.

Security Measures: - Wallets: Recognize the different kinds of wallets (cold vs. hot) and how to keep them safe. **Two-Factor Authentication (2FA)**:
To improve security, enable 2FA on your accounts.

Regulatory Environment: - Regulations: Become acquainted with the laws and regulations governing cryptocurrencies in your nation.

Legal Considerations: Make sure that cryptocurrency transactions are compliant with all applicable local laws and tax legislation. **Strategies for Trading**: - To comprehend price charts and trading signals, it is important to acquire a fundamental understanding of technical analysis.

Basis of Analysis: Examine the foundations of cryptocurrencies, taking into account the application cases, team, and technology.

How to Profit from Cryptocurrency Always.

Have Reasonable Expectations: - **Profit Potential**: Recognize that there are hazards in addition to chances for profit. Profits are not guaranteed by any technique.

Long-Term Perspective: Rather than concentrating only on short-term gains, take a long-term strategy to investing.

Create a Strategy: - Trading Plan: Establish a well-defined trading plan with defined objectives, tactics, and guidelines for risk management. - **Diversification**: Spread out your investments to lessen the impact of a single asset's underperformance and to spread risk.

Ongoing Education: - Market Trends: Keep up with industry advancements and trends so that you can modify your tactics appropriately.

Modify Approaches: Be prepared to modify your tactics in light of evolving market conditions as well as personal encounters.

Avert Emotional Investing: - Restraint: Adhere to your trading strategy and refrain from making choices influenced by feelings or market exaggeration.

Patience: Remain patient and refrain from making rash decisions based on transient market fluctuations.

How to Prevent Cryptocurrency Scams.

Investigations Completely: - Due Diligence: Before making an investment, thoroughly investigate any cryptocurrency project. Examine the project's credentials, crew, and whitepaper.

Warning Signs: Projects that make outlandish promises, lack transparency, or have faceless crews should be avoided. **Use Trusted Exchanges:** - Exchange Selection: Pick reliable, well-known cryptocurrency exchanges to trade and hold your assets on.
Security Features: Check if the exchange has a solid security record and strong security features.

Be Wary of Scams and Phishing:

- Phishing: Refrain from clicking on dubious links or giving personal information to unidentified sources. Alerts Regarding Scams: Investment plans or unsolicited offers that promise large returns with little risk should be avoided.

Confirm Information: - <u>Cross-Check</u>: Confirm the accuracy and dependability of information by cross-referencing it with data from several sources.

<u>Input from the Community</u>:
To determine the validity of initiatives and offers, get input from respectable community members and specialists.

It takes practical experience, ongoing education, and a firm grasp of investment principles to begin investing in cryptocurrencies.

You can lower risks and traverse the cryptocurrency world more skillfully if you learn the fundamentals of investing, build competence in the field, comprehend important trading factors, and keep an eye out for scams.

CHAPTER 2

Types of Cryptocurrencies

The cryptocurrency landscape is vast and diverse, with thousands of different cryptocurrencies in existence today. While Bitcoin is the most famous, many other cryptocurrencies have emerged, each with unique features and use cases. This section explores the main types of cryptocurrencies, highlighting their characteristics and the roles they play in the broader crypto ecosystem.

Bitcoin: The Pioneer

Bitcoin is the original cryptocurrency, created by an anonymous individual or group known as Satoshi Nakamoto in 2008. It was designed as a peer-to-peer electronic cash system, allowing users to send and receive payments without relying on a central authority like a bank or government.

Key Characteristics:
Decentralization: Bitcoin is run on a decentralized network, which means that no organization controls it.
Limited Supply: Since there will only ever be 21 million Bitcoins, this asset will experience deflation.
- *Security and Immutability:* Bitcoin transactions are recorded on a blockchain, a public ledger that is secure and immutable, meaning once a transaction is confirmed, it cannot be altered or reversed.
- *Store of Value:* Often referred to as "digital gold," Bitcoin is seen by many as a store of value and a hedge against inflation, much like precious metals.

Impact on the Crypto World:

Bitcoin's creation paved the way for the entire cryptocurrency industry. It demonstrated the viability of decentralized digital currencies and inspired the development of thousands of other cryptocurrencies, collectively known as "altcoins." Today, Bitcoin remains the most valuable and widely recognized cryptocurrency, often serving as the entry point for new investors and enthusiasts.

Altcoins: Ethereum, Ripple, Litecoin, and More
"Alternative coins," often known as "altcoins," are all cryptocurrency that aren't Bitcoin. While Bitcoin was designed primarily as a digital currency, many altcoins have been developed to address specific limitations of Bitcoin or to serve different purposes entirely.

Key Examples:
- Ethereum (ETH): Launched in 2015 by Vitalik Buterin, Ethereum is more than just a cryptocurrency; it is a decentralized platform

that allows developers to build and deploy smart contracts and decentralized applications (DApps). Ethereum's blockchain can be seen as a global, decentralized computer that runs code exactly as programmed, without any possibility of downtime, censorship, or fraud. Ether (ETH) is the native currency used to pay for transactions and computational services on the Ethereum network.

- **Ripple (XRP):** Ripple is both a cryptocurrency and a digital payment protocol designed for fast, low-cost international money transfers. Unlike most cryptocurrencies, Ripple is not based on blockchain technology. Instead, it uses a consensus ledger and relies on a network of independent validating servers. XRP, Ripple's native cryptocurrency, is used as a bridge currency in cross-border transactions between different fiat currencies.

- **Litecoin (LTC):** Created by Charlie Lee in 2011, Litecoin is often referred to as "the silver to Bitcoin's gold." It was designed to be a lighter, faster version of Bitcoin, with a quicker block generation time and a different hashing algorithm (Scrypt). Litecoin aims to process transactions more quickly and with lower fees, making it suitable for smaller, everyday transactions.

- **Other Notable Altcoins:** Beyond Ethereum, Ripple, and Litecoin, there are thousands of other altcoins with various purposes, ranging from privacy-focused coins like Monero (XMR) to meme-inspired tokens like Dogecoin (DOGE).

Why Altcoins Matter:
Altcoins bring innovation to the cryptocurrency space by offering new functionalities, improving upon Bitcoin's design, or catering to specific niches. They provide investors with a broader range of options and allow developers to experiment with different technologies and economic models. Some altcoins have grown significantly in value and adoption, becoming

major players in the crypto market alongside Bitcoin.

Stablecoins: Bridging the Gap

Stablecoins are a unique type of cryptocurrency designed to minimize price volatility. Unlike other cryptocurrencies, which can experience dramatic price swings, stablecoins are pegged to a stable asset, such as a fiat currency (e.g., US Dollar) or a commodity (e.g., gold). This pegging mechanism helps to stabilize their value, making them useful for everyday transactions, savings, and as a bridge between the traditional financial system and the crypto world.

Key Examples:
- **Tether** (USDT): Tether is one of the most popular stablecoins and is pegged 1:1 to the US Dollar. It is widely used in cryptocurrency trading as a stable store of value and a means of transferring funds between exchanges.

USD Coin (USDC): Managed by the Center consortium, which also includes businesses like Coinbase and Circle, USDC is another significant stablecoin that is likewise tethered to the US dollar. With frequent audits to guarantee it is entirely supported by reserves, USDC is renowned for its openness. - Dai (DAI): Dai is a decentralized stablecoin issued by the MakerDAO protocol on the Ethereum blockchain, in contrast to USDT and USDC, which are maintained centrally. Dai is a more decentralized stablecoin than other ones since it keeps its peg to the US dollar using a system of smart contracts and collateralized debt positions (CDPs).

The Importance of Stablecoins Stablecoins act as a link between the erratic cryptocurrency market and the reliable traditional currency market. They are especially helpful for remittances, traders who wish to lock in gains without switching to fiat, and as a reliable medium of exchange in areas where local currencies are unstable. In the DeFi

(Decentralized Finance) ecosystem, where they are utilized for borrowing, lending, and other financial activities, stablecoins are also quite important.

New Cryptocurrencies to Watch

The cryptocurrency market is always changing, with new tokens and projects appearing on a daily basis.

These newly popular cryptocurrencies frequently seek to solve certain issues, present cutting-edge technologies, or investigate novel applications. Some of these projects have the potential to grow into major participants in the cryptocurrency business, even if many of them may never see broad adoption. **Main Tendencies**: - DeFi Coins: A new generation of cryptocurrencies known as Decentralized Finance (DeFi) tokens allows for the decentralized provision of financial services including lending, borrowing, and trading without the need for middlemen.

Uniswap (UNI), Aave (AAVE), and Compound (COMP) are a few examples. - **NFTs and Metaverse Tokens**: As digital assets that signify ownership of rare goods or virtual real estate, non-fungible tokens (NFTs) and tokens connected to the metaverse are becoming more and more popular. Coins with a big impact on the expanding metaverse and gaming industries include tokens like Axie Infinity (AXS) and Decentraland (MANA). - **Privacy Coins:** In response to consumers' worries over privacy in the increasingly open digital world, privacy-focused cryptocurrencies like Monero (XMR) and Zcash (ZEC) are designed to offer improved anonymity and security for users. **Governance Tokens**: Voting rights in decentralized organizations or protocols grant holders the ability to shape the project's course. Maker (MKR) and Polkadot (DOT) are two examples.

The Significance of Emerging Cryptocurrencies:

The frontier of innovation in the cryptocurrency space is represented by emerging cryptocurrencies. Even while they come with greater risk, if new technologies and use cases are discovered, they also have the potential to yield substantial returns. Keeping up with new developments might give developers and investors the chance to join the next phase of the bitcoin revolution. Navigating the cryptocurrency ecosystem requires an understanding of the various cryptocurrency varieties.

Every kind of cryptocurrency has an impact on how digital finance develops in the future, from Bitcoin's innovative role to the various features of altcoins, stablecoins, and developing tokens. How to Begin Using Digital Coins For newcomers in particular, diving into the realm of cryptocurrencies can be both thrilling and intimidating. It is critical to comprehend the initial steps in order to guide you through this new territory. This section will walk you through all the important steps, such as creating a cryptocurrency wallet, selecting an exchange, purchasing your first cryptocurrency, and making sure your assets are kept safe.

CHAPTER 3

Configuring an Online Portfolio

Your entry point into the cryptocurrency world is a cryptocurrency wallet. It's an electronic device that lets you send, receive, and store cryptocurrency. Consider it your digital assets' bank account, but with better security and control.

Coin Wallet Types:

Hot Wallets: These wallets are internet-connected software-based wallets. They make quick transactions and daily use convenient. Examples include desktop wallets like Exodus and mobile apps like MetaMask and Trust Wallet. Hot wallets are easy to use, but because they are connected to the internet, they are more susceptible to hackers.

Cold Wallets: These are offline bitcoin wallets, such as paper or hardware wallets. Hardware wallets, such as the Trezor or Ledger Nano S, are tangible objects that safely hold your private keys and are impervious to cyberattacks. The safest method for long-term storage of significant quantities of cryptocurrency is thought to be using cold wallets.

Depositories versus Non-Depositories:

Custodial wallets are offered by exchanges or other businesses that act as your personal bank, holding your private keys. However, you have complete control over your private keys with non-custodial wallets, which increases security and independence.

Wallet Configuration:

Step 1:

Select Your Wallet: Choose between a cold wallet for optimal protection and a hot wallet for ease of use.

Step 2:

Download or Buy: Download the software or app from a reliable source if you're going with a hot wallet. Buy a hardware wallet directly from the manufacturer if you're using one. -

Step 3:

Make a wallet backup.

You'll be given a seed phrase—a string of 12–24 words—during the setup process, which serves as a backup for your wallet.

The seed phrase is the only method to get your money back if you misplace your wallet or device, so make sure to write it down and keep it safe.

Step 4:

Secure Your Wallet:

Don't share your private keys with anyone, create strong passwords, and turn on two-factor authentication (2FA).

Selecting a Crypto Exchange.

An exchange for cryptocurrencies is a website where you can purchase, sell, and trade them. Selecting the best exchange is essential since it influences fees, security, accessibility to other cryptocurrencies, and overall experience.

Exchange types include:

Centralized Exchanges (CEXs): These are the most popular kinds of exchanges, run by businesses that handle user money and offer a trading platform.

Binance, Coinbase, and Kraken are a few examples.

High liquidity, a large selection of cryptocurrencies, and intuitive user interfaces are provided by CEXs. But because they demand that consumers trust the exchange with their money, security becomes an issue.

DEXs (Decentralized Exchanges): Smart contracts on DEXs enable users to transact directly with one another in a decentralized environment.

Uniswap, SushiSwap, and PancakeSwap are a few instances.

DEXs give users more privacy and control over their money, but they can also be more complicated and have less liquidity for new users.

Peer-to-peer (P2P) Exchanges: By bringing buyers and sellers together directly, P2P platforms such as LocalBitcoins and Paxful enable them to bargain over terms of sale and payment. P2P exchanges come in handy in areas where access to traditional banking is restricted or where there are restrictions on cryptocurrency.

Selecting the Appropriate Exchange: - **Reputation and Security**: Examine the exchange's background, user opinions, and security protocols. Seek out exchanges with a solid reputation and good security measures, such as cold storage of funds and two-factor authentication.

Fees: Evaluate the costs associated with deposits, withdrawals, and trading on various exchanges. While some exchanges provide reduced costs, specific transactions may result in higher rates. - **Available Cryptocurrencies**:

Verify that the exchange has the coins you're looking to buy. While some exchanges focus just on well-known coins like Ethereum and Bitcoin, others provide a wider range of alternative coins.

Ease of Use: If you're new to trading cryptocurrencies, pick an exchange with an intuitive user interface. To assist new users, several exchanges additionally provide instructional materials and customer service.

Registration: -

Step 1:

Set up an account by entering your email address, coming up with a secure password, and finishing any identity verification (KYC) procedures that may be necessary.

Step 2:

Add money to your account Use a bank transfer, credit/debit card, or another cryptocurrency to add money to your exchange account.

Step 3:

Open a Trade You can begin purchasing, selling, and trading cryptocurrencies as soon as your account is funded.

Purchasing Your First Bit of Bit Coin

When your wallet is configured and an exchange is selected, you are prepared to purchase your first bitcoin. The procedure is simple, but it needs to be carefully planned in terms of budget, schedule, and tactics.

How to Purchase Cryptocurrency - Step 1: Select a Cryptocurrency: Make a decision on the cryptocurrency you wish to purchase. There are dozens of additional options, depending on your interests and risk tolerance, but Bitcoin and Ethereum are popular choices for novices due to their widespread usage and stability.

Step 2: Make a Purchase: Proceed to the trading part of your preferred exchange, pick the cryptocurrency you wish to purchase, and decide whether to put a market order—which buys it at the current market price—or a limit order, which sets the price at which you want to acquire it.

Step 3: Verify the Acquisition: Examine the specifics of your order, such as the quantity of bitcoin you're purchasing and the overall price. Once content, validate the transaction.

Step 4: Transfer to Your Wallet: It is recommended to move your just acquired bitcoin from the exchange to your own wallet for security reasons. This lowers the possibility that you may lose your money in the event that the exchange is compromised or shuts down.

Guidelines for Purchasing Cryptocurrency: - Initiate Small: Until you have more experience, it's advisable to begin with a modest investment as a newbie.

Remain Updated: The price of cryptocurrencies might fluctuate a lot. Observe news, events, and market trends related to the cryptocurrency industry. - **Diversify**: To distribute risk over a variety of assets, diversify your portfolio if you're investing in several cryptocurrencies.

Keeping Your Crypto Safe and Secure.

Making sure your cryptocurrency is secure after you've purchased it is crucial. Because cryptocurrency runs on a decentralized network, there is no central authority that can help you retrieve your wallet or private keys if you misplace them.

Optimal Methods for Maintaining and Safeguarding Your Cryptocurrency - <u>Use Cold Storage for Extended Holdings:</u>
 Use a hardware wallet or another type of cold storage if you intend to retain your Bitcoin for a long time in order to keep it offline and safe from hackers. - <u>Continually Make Wallet Backups</u>: Make sure you have several copies of the seed phrase for your wallet kept in various safe places. If your wallet is lost or compromised, this is your last chance to get your money back.
 <u>Activate Two-Factor Authentication (2FA):</u> To increase security, activate 2FA for any cryptocurrency-related accounts, including wallets and exchange accounts. <u>Watch Out for Phishing Schemes</u>: You should always double-check the URLs of websites you visit, and you should be wary of unsolicited emails or texts that request your login credentials or

private keys. <u>Remain Current on Security Procedures:</u>
Both the bitcoin market and cybercriminals' strategies are always changing. Keep up with the most recent security best practices and possible dangers.

Insurance and Custodial Services: - Consider Insured Custody Services: For significant cryptocurrency holdings, a few exchanges and outside providers offer insured custody options that give users extra piece of mind. - **Understand the Risks**: Keeping bitcoin carries danger, even with the greatest security procedures in place. Recognize these hazards and take action to reduce them as much as you can. Setting up a safe wallet, selecting the best exchange, and making your first purchase are all essential steps in getting started with cryptocurrencies.

You can enter the cryptocurrency world with confidence if you abide by these rules, which will guarantee the security of your money and the best possible experience..

50 Crypto for Beginners

CHAPTER 4

Comprehending Blockchain Technology.

Although blockchain technology is the foundation of cryptocurrencies, its applications go well beyond virtual money. Gaining an understanding of blockchain principles is essential to understanding the workings of cryptocurrencies and the wider ramifications of this innovative technology. The fundamentals of blockchain technology, its operation, the function of smart contracts and decentralized apps (DApps), and its possible future will all be covered in this part.

Fundamentals of Blockchain.

A blockchain is essentially a distributed, decentralized digital ledger that keeps track of transactions via a network of computers. Because of the way it is structured—a chain of blocks with a list of transactions in each block—the term "blockchain" was coined.

Key Features of Blockchain: - Decentralization: A blockchain is run by a network of nodes (computers) that collaborate to maintain the ledger, as opposed to traditional databases that are under the control of a single institution. Because there is no longer a need for a central authority, there is less chance of fraud or manipulation thanks to decentralization.

Transparency: Every user on the network may see every transaction that is registered on the blockchain. Users' confidence and accountability are guaranteed by this transparency. - Security: Blockchain protects data with cryptographic methods. Since a cryptographic hash connects each block to the one before it, it is practically hard to change the contents without the network noticing.

Immutability: A transaction cannot be altered or removed once it is registered on the blockchain. The data on the blockchain is dependable and trustworthy because of its immutability.

Uses Not Just for Cryptocurrency: Blockchain technology was first created to support Bitcoin, but it has since found use in a number of sectors, including voting systems, supply chain management, finance, and healthcare. Any system that needs accountability and trust can benefit from its ability to create safe, transparent, and unchangeable records.

The Operation of Blockchain.

It's useful to break down the blockchain process into its essential elements and processes in order to comprehend how it operates.

Exchanges: The first step in the blockchain process is called a transaction. A transaction, for instance, takes place in a cryptocurrency network such as Bitcoin when a user transfers a specific quantity of Bitcoin to another user. The network is notified of this transaction.

Generation of Blocks: A block is created from a collection of transactions that have all been verified by the network. A timestamp, a list of recent transactions, and a reference to the preceding block in the chain—referred to as the "previous hash"—are all included in each block.

Consensus Mechanism Validation: A block needs to be verified by the network before it can be added to the blockchain. We call this procedure reaching consensus. Various consensus techniques are used by different blockchains; the most popular ones are:

Proof of Work (PoW):

Miners, or participants, must solve challenging mathematical puzzles to validate a block using PoW, which is used by Bitcoin. Although it uses a lot of energy, this technique is very safe.

Proof of Stake (PoS):

Used by blockchains such as Ethereum 0, PoS mandates that in order to confirm transactions, validators must retain a certain quantity of the native cryptocurrency of the blockchain as collateral. PoW is not as energy-efficient as this strategy.

Incorporating into the Blockchain: The block is added to the current block chain after validation. A cryptographic hash connects the most recent block to the oldest block, guaranteeing the blockchain's continuity and integrity.

Conclusion: The transactions that are included in a block are regarded as final and irreversible once it is added. All participants will have a consistent and exact record of the events thanks to this finality.

<u>Safety and Honesty</u>: Blockchain is extremely secure since it is decentralized and uses cryptographic hashing. Any effort to modify a transaction would necessitate modifying each of the chain's subsequent blocks, which the network would identify and reject.

Decentralized Applications (DApps)

with Smart Contracts The development of smart contracts and decentralized applications (DApps), which expand the functionality of blockchains beyond simple transactions, is one of the most important developments in blockchain technology. **Clever Contracts**: Self-executing contracts, or smart contracts, have the conditions of the contract explicitly encoded into the code. When certain circumstances are satisfied, they automatically enforce and carry out the agreements without the need for middlemen.

Key Features: - Automation: Smart contracts reduce the need for manual involvement by automatically executing when criteria are satisfied. - **Transparency and Trust**: Since smart contracts are implemented on a blockchain, everyone involved can view and confirm the terms of the contract, which promotes transparency. - **Security**: Once implemented, smart contracts are unchangeable and impervious to tampering, providing fraud protection.

Smart Contract Use Cases: - **Finance**: Loans, insurance claims, and automated payments can all be handled without the assistance of banks or other financial organizations.

Supply Chain: By tracking and validating the flow of goods, smart contracts provide transparency and lower fraud.

Real Estate: Escrow services and legal middlemen are not required for the execution of property transactions and ownership transfers.

Decentralized applications, or DApps for short: DApps are programs that operate on a decentralized blockchain network as opposed to a centralized server. To construct completely decentralized services, they integrate user interfaces with smart contracts.

Main Features of DApps: - Decentralization: DApps are not governed by a single party, in contrast to traditional apps. Peer-to-peer networking allows them to function without being censored or shut down by a central authority.

Open Source: A lot of DApps are open source, which means that anybody may audit them and view their source code. This openness fosters confidence and makes community-driven growth possible. - **Token-Based**: To encourage users and developers to engage with the network, DApps frequently employ tokens as a kind of currency within their ecosystem.

DApp Examples: - Decentralized Finance (DeFi) DApps: Users can conduct financial transactions directly with platforms such as Uniswap (which facilitates decentralized trading) and Compound (which facilitates decentralized lending).

Gaming DApps: Players can acquire in-game assets that can be exchanged on blockchain markets and earn bitcoin by playing games like Axie Infinity and Decentraland.

Social DApps: Users who create and share content on decentralized social networks like Minds and Steemit are rewarded with cryptocurrency.

The Blockchain's Future.

Although blockchain technology is still in its infancy, it has the potential to revolutionize a wide range of sectors. The future of blockchain is anticipated to be shaped by a number of trends and changes as the technology continues to advance.

Performance and Scalability: Scalability is one of the issues blockchain technology is now facing. Networks can get slower and cost more to use as they get larger. On the other hand, sharding (used in Ethereum 0) and layer 2 protocols (like Lightning Network for Bitcoin) are being developed as solutions to increase scalability and performance, allowing blockchain to handle more transactions at a reduced cost. **Compatibility**: The more blockchains that are established, the more important it is that they connect and communicate with one another. Polkadot and Cosmos are two examples of interoperability solutions that are being created to provide smooth communication between various blockchains, promoting an ecosystem that is more interconnected and effective.

DeFi (Decentralized Finance) and Upward: With its decentralized alternatives to banking, lending, and trading, DeFi has already started to upend traditional finance. We should anticipate seeing increasingly complex blockchain-based financial services and solutions as DeFi develops. Beyond DeFi, blockchain could transform other industries by offering more transparent, safe, and effective systems in the government, healthcare, and supply chain management.

Control and Acceptance: Governments and regulatory agencies are paying more attention to how to control the blockchain business as it continues to garner mainstream attention. Adoption could be accelerated and given legitimacy by well-defined rules, but these must balance consumer protection with innovation promotion.

Impact on the Environment: Blockchain's effects on the environment have drawn a lot of attention, especially in relation to energy-intensive consensus techniques like Proof of Work.

To lessen the carbon footprint of blockchain networks, the industry is looking into more environmentally friendly options including Proof of Stake and other energy-efficient consensus techniques. **Web3's Ascent**: Web3, or the decentralized web made possible by blockchain technology, is the next stage of the internet. Web3 replaces traditional servers and middlemen with decentralized networks, giving consumers ownership over their data and online identities.

This change may completely change the way we use the internet by providing increased security, privacy, and freedom. Beyond merely serving as the basis for cryptocurrencies, blockchain technology is a revolutionary force that has the power to completely change industries and the way we interact with digital systems. You can recognize the significant influence that blockchain technology is expected to have in the upcoming years by being aware of the fundamentals of the technology, how it functions, the function of smart contracts and DApps, and its future possibilities.

CHAPTER 5

Buying, Selling, and Trading Cryptocurrency.

While there are many advantages to trading and long-term investing with cryptocurrencies, there are also considerable risks associated with this volatile and quickly developing industry. It's critical to comprehend the fundamentals of cryptocurrency trading, market analysis, the distinctions between long-term investing and day trading, and risk management techniques in order to properly traverse this area.

To assist you in making wise judgments in the world of cryptocurrency, this section will walk you through these crucial topics.

How to Trade Cryptocurrencies 101

Buying and selling digital assets like Bitcoin, Ethereum, and other altcoins in order to profit from price swings is known as cryptocurrency trading. The cryptocurrency market is always open and offers trading opportunities, in contrast to regular stock markets. Still, traders must exercise discipline and vigilance in this 24/7 market.

Types of Trading Cryptocurrencies: **Spot Trading**: This is the simplest type of trading; you purchase a cryptocurrency, keep it until its value rises, and then sell it to make a profit. Real-time transactions with instantaneous settlement are involved.

Margin Trading: To trade bigger positions than your actual balance permits, you must borrow money from an exchange. This is a high-risk, high-reward approach since it has the potential to magnify both gains and losses. **Futures Trading**: With futures contracts, dealers can purchase or dispose of an asset at a fixed price at a future date. This kind of trading entails projecting a cryptocurrency's future price movement and can be used for hedging or speculation.

Options Trading: Options provide investors the choice, but not the obligation, to purchase or sell cryptocurrencies within a predetermined window of time at a given price. This tactic is frequently employed as a loss hedging technique.

Principles Crucial to Trading: -

Liquidity: The degree to which a cryptocurrency's price can be changed by buying or selling it easily. High liquidity is ideal since it facilitates speedy transactions and steady pricing. Volatility: The extent of price fluctuation of a cryptocurrency over a given period of time. High volatility raises the possibility of big losses even if it can also result in sizable winnings.

Types of Orders: - Market Order: Completes a trade right away at the going rate.

Limit Order: Provides greater control over the deal by executing it at a predetermined price or above. - **Stop-Loss Order**: This limits losses by automatically selling a cryptocurrency when its price hits a specific level. **Getting Started with Trading:** - <u>**Select a Platform**</u>: Pick a cryptocurrency exchange that provides the functionality and trading possibilities you want in addition to the required tools. **Experience with Paper Trading**: Demo accounts are available on many platforms, allowing you to practice trading without having to risk real money.

Start Small: It's advisable to begin with a little investment as a novice and to progressively increase it as you gain confidence and experience.

Examining the Cryptocurrency Market Analyzing price movements and having a thorough understanding of market trends are essential for successful bitcoin trading. Technical analysis and fundamental analysis are the two primary methods used to analyze the cryptocurrency market.

Fundamental Analysis (FA): In fundamental analysis, the intrinsic worth of a cryptocurrency is assessed using a number of different criteria, including: **Technology and Innovation**: Evaluating the blockchain's application, future acceptance, and underlying technology. - **Team and Development**: Examining the project's advancement as well as the development team's reputation and background.

Market Demand and Supply:

Assessing the amount of demand as well as the supply of the cryptocurrency, taking into account scarcity (such as the limited supply of Bitcoin) and issuance rate. - Partnerships and Community Support: Taking into account the size and activity of a cryptocurrency's user community, as well as the strength of its partnerships and collaborations.

Regulatory Environment: Being aware of how laws and court cases may affect the future expansion of cryptocurrencies.

Technical Analysis (TA): In order to forecast future price movements, technical analysis examines price charts and data indicators. Important elements of technical analysis consist of:

Price Charts: Using different chart types (such as candlestick, line, and bar) to analyze historical price data and spot trends and patterns.

Support and Resistance Levels: A cryptocurrency's tendency to reverse course (support) or experience selling pressure (resistance) at certain price points.

Moving Averages (MA): Determine trends by averaging a cryptocurrency's price over a given time frame. The 50-day and 200-day moving averages are examples of common moving averages. - An indicator of momentum that assesses overbought or oversold circumstances by tracking the rate and direction of price changes.

Bollinger Bands: A volatility indicator that looks for possible price breakouts or reversals using a moving average with upper and lower bands. Integrating TA and FA: Although some traders have a preference for one approach over another, a more thorough understanding of the market can be obtained by combining fundamental and technical analysis. For example, you could use technical analysis to determine the best times to enter and exit cryptocurrency trades, and utilize fundamental analysis to find promising coins for long-term investments.

Day trading versus long-term investing.

Day trading and long-term investing are two distinct ways to make money in the bitcoin space. Every strategy has benefits and drawbacks, so the best option will rely on your objectives, level of risk tolerance, and availability of time.

HoDLing, or long-term investing: Long-term investing, sometimes known as "HODLing" (a phrase derived from the misspelling of "hold"), is the practice of purchasing and retaining cryptocurrencies for a considerable amount of time, typically years, in the hopes that their value would rise.

Benefits: - Lower Stress: Long-term investors experience less emotional strain from regular trading since they are less worried with daily price swings.

High Return Potential: Due to the considerable growth that cryptocurrencies like Bitcoin and Ethereum have demonstrated over time, long-term investing may be profitable.

Less Time-Intensive: Long-term investment is appropriate for people who have less time to devote to trading because it doesn't necessitate continuous market monitoring.

Risks: - Market Volatility: Due to the extreme volatility of cryptocurrencies, long-term investors need to be ready for large price fluctuations.

Regulatory Changes: Over time, the value of cryptocurrencies may be impacted by the changing regulatory environment. **Technological Risks**: The success of a long-term investment is contingent upon the underlying technology's ongoing advancement and uptake.

Day Trading: Buying and selling cryptocurrencies in a single day in order to profit from transient price fluctuations is known as day trading. This approach necessitates rapid decision-making, a thorough understanding of technical analysis, and ongoing market monitoring. <u>**Benefits**</u>: - Quick Profits: Day traders can benefit quickly by utilizing brief price fluctuations.

Taking Advantage of Volatility: The daily fluctuations in the bitcoin market offer a plethora of trading chances.

High Liquidity: Day traders frequently work with cryptocurrencies that are extremely liquid, making it easy to enter and exit positions quickly.

Risks: - High Stress: Because day trading is a fast-paced technique, it can be emotionally taxing and demands continual market attention.

Potential for Significant Losses: Day traders run the danger of suffering large losses, particularly if they employ leverage.

Time-Consuming: Constant market monitoring and a large time commitment are necessary for successful day trading. Selecting Between the Pair: Your time constraints, risk tolerance, and financial objectives will all influence your decision between day trading and long-term investing.

A hybrid method is chosen by some investors who keep a long-term investing portfolio and occasionally day trade in order to take advantage of market opportunities.

Handling Cryptocurrency Investment

Risks Given the inherent volatility of the cryptocurrency market, risk management is an essential component of trading and investing in cryptocurrencies. Even seasoned traders may experience substantial losses in the absence of effective risk management techniques.

Diversification: To lessen the impact of a single asset's bad performance, diversify your assets over a number of cryptocurrencies. One way to reduce the risk arising from the volatility of specific cryptocurrencies is to diversify your investments.

How to Set Stop-Loss Orders: In order to reduce possible losses, a stop-loss order automatically sells a cryptocurrency when its price drops to a specific threshold. It is especially helpful for traders who are unable to keep an eye on the market all the time. By establishing a stop-loss, you can make sure that you get out of a trade before the losses get too big.

Sizing of Position: The quantity of capital you devote to a specific trade or investment is referred to as position sizing. You may avoid risking too much of your capital on a single trade by using proper position sizing. It's generally advised to avoid risking more than 1% to 2% of your entire portfolio on any one trade. Steer clear of FOMO (fear of missing out): Fear of losing out on possible gains, or FOMO, can cause impulsive decisions. One example of this would be purchasing a cryptocurrency at its highest price. Follow your trading or investing plan and refrain from making choices based on your feelings or the buzz around the market to prevent FOMO.

Remaining Up to Date: The bitcoin market is always changing as new innovations, rules, and technology appear on a daily basis. Making educated decisions and avoiding potential pitfalls requires keeping up with the most recent news and trends.

Timely Evaluations of Portfolios: You may evaluate the success of your investments and make any required modifications by routinely monitoring your portfolio. Rebalancing your portfolio, extracting profits, or reducing losses on underperforming investments could all be part of this.

Using Cold Storage for Extended Periods of Time:

Keeping a sizable percentage of your cryptocurrencies in an offline wallet, or cold wallet, lowers the danger of theft or loss from hacking for long-term investors. An additional layer of security is offered by cold storage, particularly for big holdings. Comprehending and Handling Credit: By borrowing money to expand their trading position, traders can use leverage to maximize their prospective returns.

CHAPTER 6

Mining Cryptocurrencies

A key function of many cryptocurrency networks, especially those that use Proof of Work (PoW) as its consensus method, is crypto mining.
Even though it has grown from a specialized hobby to a sizable industry, cryptocurrency mining may be difficult and resource-intensive. This section will discuss the definition of cryptocurrency mining, the distinctions between Proof of Stake and Proof of Work, how to start a mining business, and if cryptocurrency mining is still profitable in the current market.

What is Mining Crypto?

The process of creating new cryptocurrency coins or tokens, verifying transactions, and adding them to the blockchain is known as crypto mining. Mining is essential to preserving the security and integrity of decentralized networks.

How Mining Operates:

Transaction Validation: On a blockchain network, transactions are collected into blocks by users. Miners compete to solve challenging mathematical puzzles in order to validate this block.

Cryptographic Puzzle: To answer this mathematical conundrum, which is also known as a cryptographic puzzle, a substantial amount of processing power is needed. The first miner to solve the riddle adds the block to the blockchain and receives transaction fees from the block as well as freshly created cryptocurrency (like Bitcoin).

Decentralization and Security: The blockchain is kept under no single entity's control thanks to mining. The network is protected from assaults by the computational effort needed to validate transactions, which makes it difficult and expensive for bad actors to change the blockchain.

Principles of Mining: - Hash Rate: A miner's processing capacity is gauged by this. The likelihood of cracking the cryptographic puzzle and winning rewards rises with higher hash rates.

Mining Hardware: The kind of hardware utilized has a big influence on how efficient mining is. For some cryptocurrencies, such as Bitcoin, miners use Application-Specific Integrated Circuits (ASICs) or high-performance GPUs (Graphics Processing Units).

Energy Consumption: One of the most important and expensive parts of mining is energy consumption because it takes a lot of electricity to power the equipment.

Evidence of Stake vs. Proof of Work

A key component of how blockchains agree on the network's current state is the consensus process.

Two of the most often utilized consensus techniques in cryptocurrencies are Proof of Work (PoW) and Proof of Stake (PoS). Workproof (PoW):

The original proof-of-work (PoW) consensus algorithm underlies Bitcoin and numerous other cryptocurrencies. In Proof of Work (PoW) mining, participants compete to solve cryptographic puzzles; the first person to do so adds the block to the blockchain and earns a reward. PoW characteristics:

Security: Because it takes a lot of computing power to change the blockchain, PoW is extremely safe. **Energy-Intensive**: Because PoW uses a significant amount of electricity, there are environmental issues.

Decentralization: PoW can lead to centralization if a small number of powerful entities control most of the hash rate, but it can also be quite decentralized if mining power is distributed among many players. **Stake Proof (PoS)**: PoS is a different, more energy-efficient consensus method. Validators are selected to generate new blocks based on the quantity of cryptocurrency they own and are prepared to "stake" as collateral, as opposed to competing to solve problems.

Features of PoS: - Energy Efficiency: Because PoS doesn't rely on processing power, it uses a lot less energy than PoW. Security: Proof of Stake (PoS) is safe as long as the majority of stake is owned by trustworthy participants. A validator runs the danger of forfeiting the cryptocurrency they have staked. - **Decentralization**: PoS can encourage decentralization by bringing down the entry barrier, but if large holders control the staking process, it could also encourage centralization.

What Is Superior?

The decision between PoW and PoS is influenced by a number of variables, such as the required degree of decentralization, security requirements, and environmental considerations. Although PoW is thought to be more reliable and secure, PoS provides a more accessible and long-lasting substitute.

Starting a Mining Business

A crypto mining operation needs to be set up with careful planning, a substantial investment, and continuous management. Here's a simple how-to for getting going. **Selecting Your Cryptocurrency**: Selecting the cryptocurrency you wish to mine is the first step. The kind of gear you require and the possible profitability of your business will depend on this choice. While Bitcoin is the most well-known cryptocurrency, mining possibilities are also available for other cryptocurrencies including Litecoin, Monero, and Ethereum (before it switched to PoS).

Get Hardware for Mining: Selecting the right hardware is essential to your mining operation's success. The two main choices are:

Application-Specific Integrated Circuits (ASICs):

Extremely specialized equipment made to mine particular coins, mostly Bitcoin. ASICs can be costly, but they are strong and efficient. Graphics Processing Units, or GPUs): GPUs are more adaptable than ASICs and are frequently used for altcoin mining.
Numerous coins can be mined by them.
They are, nevertheless, often less potent than ASICs.

Configure the Software for Mining:
To link your hardware to the blockchain network after purchasing it, you'll need mining software. A few well-liked mining software choices are EasyMiner, BFGMiner, and CGMiner. You can monitor performance, manage your mining

equipment, and be paid with the aid of these apps.

Sign Up for a Mining Pool:
Mining on its own can be difficult because of competition, particularly in big networks like Bitcoin. By pooling your computing power with others', you can increase your chances of winning prizes by joining a mining pool. Upon the pool's successful block mining, each member receives a payout according to their respective participation.

Take placement Into Account: Because mining operations use a lot of electricity, the placement of your mining setup is quite important. Setting your shop in an area with cheap electricity and a reliable power source is ideal. Some miners take temperature into account as well, since colder climates might minimize the need for costly cooling systems.

Determine Expenses and Earnings:
It's crucial to figure out the expenditures before you start mining, including those for gear, electricity, upkeep, and other operating charges. Based on the hash rate of your setup, the cost of

electricity, and the difficulty of mining the selected cryptocurrency right now, use online calculators to calculate your possible earnings.

Sustain and Improve Your Business: Regular maintenance is crucial to ensuring optimal performance once your mining operation is up and running. This entails keeping an eye on hardware temperatures, upgrading software, and thinking about upgrading hardware when mining complexity rises or new, more capable hardware becomes accessible.

Is Mining Cryptocurrency Lucrative?

A number of variables affect the profitability of cryptocurrency mining, such as the cost of the coin, the difficulty of the mining process, the cost of power, and the effectiveness of your mining equipment. **Factors Affecting Profitability:** - Cryptocurrency Price: Your mining profits are directly impacted by the value of the cryptocurrency you are mining. While low prices may result in losses, high prices might generate large profits. Mining <u>Difficulty</u>: The difficulty of mining rises with the number of miners on the network, demanding more processing power and decreasing the likelihood of successfully mining a block.

Electricity Costs: One of the biggest outlays is electricity because mining uses a lot of energy. Profitability can be significantly increased by reducing these expenses.

Hardware Efficiency: Your business will be more profitable if your hardware is more efficient, or has a greater hash rate per watt. Upgrading to newer, more efficient gear on a regular basis can support profitability.

Competitiveness Estimators: With a number of online tools, miners can project their possible earnings depending on system specifications, electricity rates, and network conditions as of right now. As examples, consider:

WhatToMine: Based on the hash rate of your gear, this tool analyzes the profitability of mining several cryptocurrencies.

CryptoCompare: Provides a mining calculator that estimates earnings by accounting for other variables such as electricity expenses.

Difficulties and Perils: - Market Volatility: Mining profits can fluctuate due to the very volatile nature of cryptocurrency values. A steep price decline might make mining unprofitable. - **Increasing Difficulty**: Mining becomes more challenging as more participants join a network, necessitating the use of more sophisticated technology and more electricity.

Regulatory Risks: The viability and profitability of mining may be impacted by changes in governmental legislation, particularly those pertaining to the use of cryptocurrencies or power. - **Environmental Concerns**: Because mining requires a lot of energy, there are plans for laws that would lessen the impact on the environment.

Result: Although it needs a large initial investment, careful planning, and continuous management, cryptocurrency mining can be financially rewarding.

To increase their chances of success, miners need to stay up to date on market trends, technological improvements, and legislative developments as the cryptocurrency landscape changes over time.

CHAPTER 7

Privacy and Security with Cryptocurrency

Security and privacy concerns are growing along with the use of cryptocurrencies. Cryptocurrencies come with new risks in addition to their many benefits, like decentralization and borderless transactions. In the digital era, protecting your capital and maintaining your privacy requires understanding popular cryptocurrency scams, implementing best practices for asset security, and investigating coins with a privacy focus.

Typical Crypto Scams and How to Stay Away from Them.

The decentralized and comparatively uncontrolled characteristics of cryptocurrencies have rendered the market susceptible to various fraudulent activities. Crypto users need to be aware and on guard because these frauds can be quite convincing and complex.

Phishing scams: (1)

Phishing is the practice of pretending to be reputable organizations in order to deceive consumers into disclosing their passwords, secret keys, or other sensitive information. Fraudsters frequently create phony websites, emails, or social media profiles that seem real.

How to Avoid:

For extra precaution, turn on two-factor authentication (2FA), double-check URLs before inputting critical information, and never click on dubious links. Verify the provenance of any email or message you get requesting your personal information by getting in touch with the organization through legitimate methods.

Pyramid and Ponzi schemes: Rather than receiving payments from real profits, early investors in Ponzi schemes receive returns from the funds of later investors. In a similar vein, pyramid schemes make big promises about profits only to those who successfully recruit new members—not through real investments or commercial endeavors.

How to Avoid: Steer clear of investing possibilities that offer little to no risk and assured or exceptionally high profits. Prior to making an investment, always do extensive research. You should also be wary of programs that prioritize hiring over the real good or service.

Idle Coin Offerings, or Fake ICOs:

Often, scammers use copying already-existing, successful initial coin offerings (ICOs) or completely made-up ones to launch bogus cryptocurrency projects. They entice investors with the prospect of large returns, but after the initial coin offering (ICO) ends, they vanish with the money.

How to Avoid: Always read the whitepaper, the track record, and the team behind an initial coin offering (ICO). Look for comments from the community and recommendations from reliable sources. Steer careful of ventures with unidentified teams or ambiguous business plans.

Attacks using Social Engineering:
Social engineering is the practice of coercing people into disclosing private information. This can happen in a number of ways, including impersonation, phony customer service, and instilling a sense of urgency.

How to Avoid: Be wary of unsolicited correspondence, particularly if it asks for private information. Make sure everyone you engage with is who they say they are, and never give out your passwords or private keys.

Concealed Wallets and Exchanges:
Fraudsters fabricate phony cryptocurrency wallets or exchanges that seem authentic. The crooks take possession of the assets when users enter their secret keys or deposit money.

<u>Avoid</u>: Make sure you only use trusted and well-established wallets and exchangers.

Make sure the website is using HTTPS and examine reviews and community comments to confirm the platform's legitimacy. Don't download wallet software from unreliable websites. Schemes for **Pumps and Dumping:** Pump and dump strategies include a group of people heavily pushing a coin, falsely inflating its price. When the price rises, they profitably sell their holdings, causing other investors to lose money when the price plummets. - **How to Avoid**: Watch out for unexpected price increases in lesser-known cryptocurrencies, particularly if they're coupled with aggressive marketing on forums or social media. Invest only in businesses with strong fundamentals; stay away from hype.

Securing Cryptocurrency

Best Practices Because blockchain transactions are irreversible, protecting your cryptocurrency is essential. You have no legal remedy if your assets are stolen or lost. By putting strong security procedures in place, you can guard your money against loss and illegal access. Employ Hardware Wallets: Ledger and Trezor are examples of hardware wallets that keep your private keys offline and are hence impervious to internet hacker attempts.

They rank among the most secure methods for keeping cryptocurrency. **Tip:** To prevent tampering devices, always buy hardware wallets from the manufacturer or an approved reseller.

Turn on two-factor authentication (2FA): By requiring a second form of verification (such as a code from an app like Google Authenticator) in addition to your password, 2FA strengthens the security of your accounts.

Tip: Steer clear of SMS-based 2FA whenever you can because SIM swapping attacks can exploit it. Use hardware-based 2FA techniques or authenticator applications as an alternative.

Take Care of Your Personal Keys: The most important piece of information you have in order to access your cryptocurrency is your private key. Never give it to anyone, and think about keeping it somewhere safe, such as a paper wallet kept in a safe or a hardware wallet. - **Tip**: Make numerous secure backups of your private keys, such as encrypted USB devices or paper copies kept in various physical locations.

Always Update Your Software: Update your operating systems, antivirus programs, and wallets frequently to guard against the newest security flaws.

Tip: Make sure your software is updated automatically to stay up to current on the newest security threats.

Use Caution When Using Public WiFi: Steer clear of using public Wi-Fi to access your bitcoin accounts as it might be unreliable and vulnerable to hackers. **Tip**: Encrypt your internet connection with a Virtual Private Network (VPN) if you must access your accounts while on the go.

Make Use of Strong Passwords: Make sure each of your accounts has a strong, distinct password, and think about storing and managing them safely with a password manager.

Tip: A strong password usually consists of a mix of special characters, digits, and upper- and lowercase letters. Don't use information that can be guessed, such as birth dates or everyday terms.

Consistently Check Your Accounts: Make sure to often monitor your accounts for any unusual or unauthorized activity. You can minimize possible losses more quickly if you identify a problem early on. - **Tip**: Configure alerts on your accounts to get notified when there's any strange activity or attempt to log in.

Cryptocurrency Privacy Coins and Anonymity.

Although the majority of cryptocurrencies, including Bitcoin, provide some degree of pseudonymity, they are not completely anonymous. Every transaction is documented on the blockchain and, given sufficient information, may be linked to specific people. The goals of privacy coins are to safeguard financial privacy and improve user anonymity.

What are Coins for Privacy? Cryptocurrencies called "privacy coins" are made with characteristics that improve user privacy by hiding transactional information. Advanced cryptographic techniques are employed by these coins to conceal data, including transaction amounts, sender and recipient addresses, and occasionally even the actual transaction.

Common Private Coins: - XMR (Monero): Among the most well-known privacy coins is Monero. It makes use of methods such as stealth addresses, ring signatures, and Ring Confidential Transactions (RingCT) to make sure that amounts are hidden and transactions are untraceable.

Zcash (ZEC): Zcash provides optional privacy features via "shielded" transactions, which obscure transaction data while preserving the blockchain's integrity via a cryptographic technique known as zk-SNARKs.

Dash (DASH): Dash offers a feature called PrivateSend that anonymizes transactions by using a coin-mixing service, making transaction histories harder to find.

How Privacy Coins Operate: To guarantee anonymity, privacy coins usually combine the following methods: - **Signature Rings**: a technique in which a transaction is signed by a number of potential signers, making it challenging to identify the true signer. It is Monero who uses this method.

Stealth Addresses: This method keeps payments from being associated with a specific receiver by having the recipient use a unique address for every transaction.

Coin Mixing: A technique in which a number of transactions are merged and subsequently dispersed, hiding the funds' initial source. The Private Send function of Dash uses this technique.

Zero-Knowledge Proofs: A cryptographic technique wherein a party can demonstrate to another that they are aware of a value without actually disclosing the value. This is utilized in the protected transactions of Zcash.

Privacy vs. Anonymity: Knowing the distinction between privacy and anonymity in the context of cryptocurrency is crucial:

Privacy: is used to describe the capacity to transact without disclosing one's identity. The goal of privacy coins is to achieve anonymity by hiding transaction information.

Privacy: This refers to preventing unauthorized parties from accessing or discovering personal information. Bitcoin provides a certain amount of anonymity, but privacy coins go one step further by hiding transaction information on the blockchain.

Moral and Legal Aspects to Be Considered:

Although privacy coins offer increased secrecy and privacy, authorities are keeping a close eye on them because of worries about possible illicit uses including money laundering and tax fraud. Certain exchanges have removed privacy coins from their lists in order to adhere to legal mandates.

Consideration: Users should assess the advantages of privacy against the possible hazards of breaking rules, as well as the legal ramifications of utilizing privacy coins in their country.

Cryptocurrency's Prospects for Privacy:
The future of privacy coins is still up in the air as governments and regulatory agencies continue to create frameworks for cryptocurrencies. Nonetheless, there will probably always be a need for financial privacy, which will spur innovation in this field.

The difficulty will be striking a balance between privacy and legal compliance, which could result in the development of new technologies that improve privacy while still adhering to the law. Privacy and security are crucial when working with cryptocurrency. You may guard against fraud and theft by being aware of prevalent scams and implementing best practices for asset security. Furthermore, users who want even more anonymity have an alternative with privacy coins, but they should be aware of the legal environment in which these assets are situated.

being up to date and vigilant regarding security and privacy as the crypto industry develops.

CHAPTER 8

Global Regulations Regarding Cryptocurrencies

As cryptocurrencies continue to evolve, their potential to reshape the financial landscape and influence global economic systems becomes increasingly evident.
Understanding emerging trends, the role of crypto in the global economy, potential challenges, and future predictions can provide insights into how cryptocurrencies might develop over the coming years.
Law and Regulation Concerns The regulatory environment surrounding cryptocurrencies is changing quickly as authorities and nations try to handle the special opportunities and problems that come with digital assets. To manage the legal complexity and assure compliance, investors and users must have a thorough

understanding of cryptocurrency rules, legal issues, and tax ramifications.

Global Regulations Regarding Cryptocurrencies

Different countries have different rules regarding cryptocurrencies, which reflects their varying views on digital assets, financial innovation, and risk management.

An outline of how the main regions are handling bitcoin legislation is provided below:
United States: - Agencies Regulating: The Securities and Exchange Commission (SEC), the Commodity Futures Trading Commission (CFTC), and the Financial Crimes Enforcement Network (FinCEN) are among the U.S. institutions that oversee cryptocurrency trading. FinCEN handles compliance with anti-money laundering (AML) regulations, the CFTC controls commodity futures, and the SEC is in charge of securities laws.

Instructions: Exchanges and wallet providers that deal in cryptocurrencies must register as Money Services Businesses (MSBs), follow Know Your Customer (KYC) guidelines, and comply with AML laws. In addition, the SEC has enforced compliance with securities rules for Initial Coin Offerings (ICOs) that are considered securities offerings.

New Advancements:

The United States is currently in the process of drafting new laws to deal with new concerns like decentralized finance (DeFi) and stablecoins. As legislators work to strike a balance between investor protection and innovation, the regulatory landscape is always changing.

European Union: - Agencies for Regulation: Two important EU regulators are the European Central Bank (ECB) and the European Securities and Markets Authority (ESMA). To offer a thorough framework for regulating cryptocurrencies, the European Commission has proposed the Markets in Crypto-Assets (MiCA) regulation.

Instructions: The goal of the MiCA law is to standardize regulations on topics including market manipulation, stablecoins, and providers of services for digital assets among EU members. Additionally, wallet providers and cryptocurrency exchanges must comply with AML and KYC regulations.

New Advancements: In order to address particular issues like taxes on crypto assets and anti-money laundering protocols, the EU is now developing further rules. When the MiCA regulation is completely put into effect, more uniformity and clarity should be available throughout the region.

China in the Asia-Pacific region: China has imposed strict regulations on cryptocurrencies, outlawing cryptocurrency mining, Initial Coin Offerings (ICOs), and trading. The development of the nation's central bank digital currency (CBDC) and preservation of financial stability are its top priorities. - Japan: Japan has taken a more proactive approach, establishing a regulatory framework that includes exchange license requirements and acknowledging cryptocurrencies as legitimate property. In Japan, the Financial Services Agency (FSA) is in charge of regulating cryptocurrencies.

Korea: Regulations enacted in South Korea mandate that cryptocurrency exchanges follow KYC and AML procedures. In addition, the nation is thinking about taking more steps to control the cryptocurrency market in addition to investigating the creation of a central bank digital currency (CBDC).

Additional Areas: - Australia: The legal climate in Australia is comparatively welcoming to cryptocurrencies. Crypto exchanges must register with the Australian Transaction Reports and Analysis Centre (AUSTRAC) and abide by AML and KYC guidelines. - **India**: India's position on cryptocurrencies has changed over time, including periods of proposed restrictions and unclear legal status. Recent events suggest that rather than a complete prohibition, digital assets may soon be regulated.

Worldwide Patterns: - Normalization Initiatives: Global guidelines for cryptocurrency regulation are being developed by international groups like the Financial Action Task Force (FATF), with a focus on AML and counter-terrorism funding (CTF) measures.

CBDCs: In order to incorporate innovative digital currencies into the established financial system while preserving regulatory oversight, numerous nations are investigating or testing central bank digital currencies, or CBDCs.

Legal Things Crypto Investors Should Know.

To maintain compliance and reduce any legal risks, cryptocurrency investors must be aware of a number of legal issues.

Cryptocurrency Laws: - Currency vs. Property: Cryptocurrencies are categorized as property rather than money in certain jurisdictions. Their legal rights, property laws, and financial rules are all impacted by this classification.

Securities Legislation: Certain tokens and cryptocurrencies might be deemed securities by local legislation, necessitating adherence to securities rules. Investors must ascertain whether a specific cryptocurrency is subject to securities laws and follow any applicable rules.

Protection of Consumers: - Prevention of Fraud: Investors need to exercise caution when it comes to fraud and scams. In order to combat fraud and deceptive tactics, legal frameworks frequently incorporate consumer protection measures, albeit enforcement varies by region.

Legitimate Action: It is crucial to comprehend the legal channels open to dispute resolution and to pursue legal action in fraud or contract violations. This could entail filing a lawsuit in court or interacting with regulatory agencies.

Terms of Service: - Contractual Agreements: Investors should carefully read the terms of service and user agreements before using cryptocurrency exchanges, wallets, or other services. These agreements delineate the respective rights and obligations of the parties involved and may have significant provisions about dispute resolution, liability, and account management. - **Contract Smarts:** Investors should make sure they are aware of the terms and conditions included into any agreements or transactions incorporating smart contracts. Despite being self-executing, smart contracts could still need to be interpreted and enforced by the law.

Adherence to Regulations: - Accreditation and Registration: Crypto companies and service providers may need to apply for licenses or register with regulatory bodies in certain areas. Investors must confirm that the platforms they utilize are compliant with local laws and understand the regulatory status of those platforms.

Reporting Requirements: Investors may be required to report certain information about their cryptocurrency holdings and transactions, depending on the jurisdiction. Remaining up to date with these regulations can help guarantee compliance and prevent legal problems.

Tax Repercussions of Cryptocurrency

Trading and Holding Each country has its own tax laws pertaining to cryptocurrencies, but similar elements include how gains and losses are handled and the necessity of reporting.

Tax on Capital Gains:
Events Subject to Tax: Capital gains tax is imposed on cryptocurrency transactions in a number of nations.
This is relevant if you trade or sell cryptocurrency for a profit. When a cryptocurrency is sold, traded, or exchanged, it is when the taxable event happens.

Determining Gains:

You must figure out the difference between the cryptocurrency's acquisition price (cost basis) and sale price in order to compute capital gains. Generally, gains are classified as either long-term or short-term, and the tax rate that applies depends on how long the gain is held.

Damages: Investments in cryptocurrencies often result in capital losses that can be utilized to offset capital gains, lowering the total tax obligation. Depending on local laws, you might occasionally be able to offset losses against other forms of income.

Tax on Income: - Investment and Mining: The money you make from mining or staking cryptocurrency is normally taxed. The taxable amount is typically determined using the cryptocurrency's fair market value at the time of receipt. - Forks and Airdrops: Bitcoin obtained through forks or airdrops would potentially be taxable as income. At the time of receipt, the value of the recently acquired cryptocurrency is normally considered as taxable income.

Requirements for Reporting: - **Disclosures**: Taxpayers are required by law in several nations to disclose their bitcoin holdings and transactions. This could entail filing tax returns with transaction information, capital gains, and income from cryptocurrency-related activities disclosed.

Keeping Records: For tax reporting purposes, it is essential to keep precise records of all bitcoin transactions, including the dates, amounts, and parties involved. This makes it easier to calculate gains, losses, and income and helps to ensure compliance.

Cross-Border Transactions: - International Considerations: The tax ramifications of transnational bitcoin transactions can be complicated. Regarding the taxes of foreign transactions, different nations may have different laws, thus it's critical to comprehend the pertinent laws in each jurisdiction.

Legal Agreements: Tax treaties between some nations and cryptocurrency investors may have an impact on how cryptocurrency assets are taxed, especially for those with cross-border holdings. A tax expert's advice can be very helpful in navigating these issues.

Maintaining Compliance: - Advice: It is important to speak with a tax professional or accountant who is experienced about cryptocurrency taxation due to the complexity and variety of cryptocurrency tax rules.

They can guarantee that local laws are followed and offer advice that is customized for your particular circumstance. Being informed of the legal and regulatory environment surrounding cryptocurrencies is necessary.

To maintain compliance and safeguard their interests, investors and users must be aware of cryptocurrency laws, regulations, and tax ramifications.

Staying educated and getting competent counsel can help you manage legal risks and make the most out of your strategy of investing in and using cryptocurrencies as the regulatory landscape changes.

CHAPTER 9

The future of virtual currencies.

Cryptocurrency Trends The emergence of digital currencies issued by central banks (CBDCs): Globally, central banks are investigating or creating their own virtual currencies. The goal of digital national currencies, or CBDCs, is to bring together the advantages of digital trade and the dependability of fiat money. - Instances: Notable examples are the digital euro issued by the European Central Bank and the digital yuan (e-CNY) issued by China. These programs aim to improve the effectiveness of economic policy, financial inclusion, and payment efficiency. Result: CBDCs have the potential to improve monetary policy instruments for central banks, lessen dependency on private cryptocurrencies, and facilitate more effective cross-border payments.

Combining Conventional and Alternative Finance:
The old financial systems are becoming more and more integrated with cryptocurrencies. Blockchain technology is being investigated by banks and other financial organizations for a number of applications, such as asset management, clearing and settlement, and international payments. Instances: Trading desks and investment funds are only two examples of the cryptocurrency-related services and products that major financial institutions like JPMorgan and Goldman Sachs have introduced.

Result: Increased integration may result in cryptocurrencies being adopted more widely and being accepted by the general public, closing the gap between traditional and digital money.

Decentralized Finance's (DeFi) Growth:
DeFi is the word for a group of blockchain-based financial apps and services that function without the need for conventional

middlemen. Numerous services for decentralized lending, borrowing, trading, and yield farming have emerged in this rapidly expanding market. - <u>Instances</u>: Prominent DeFi applications that offer customers decentralized financial services include Uniswap, Aave, and Compound. - <u>Result</u>: DeFi raises questions regarding security, regulation, and market stability but it also has the potential to democratize access to financial services, reduce prices, and boost financial innovation.

Blockchain Interoperability Development:

The capacity of various blockchain networks to communicate and interact with one another is referred to as blockchain interoperability. The goal of interoperability solutions is to improve blockchain ecosystems' functionality and efficiency. - <u>Instances</u>: The goal of projects like Cosmos and Polkadot is to facilitate data sharing and cross-chain interactions. - <u>Result</u>: More smooth and integrated blockchain ecosystems might result from improved interoperability, which would encourage innovation and make cryptocurrencies and decentralized apps easier to use.

Cryptocurrency's Place in the World

Economy Financial Involvement: Financial services could be made available by cryptocurrencies to the unbanked and underbanked people around the world. In areas with little banking infrastructure, digital currencies and blockchain technology can provide access to financial services.

Example: Underprivileged groups in underdeveloped nations already have access to money thanks to crypto-based solutions like mobile wallets and remittance services.

Result: Through increased access to credit, savings, and investment opportunities, financial inclusion may boost the economy, raise living standards, and lessen poverty.

Payment System Innovation: Blockchain technologies and cryptocurrencies are propelling innovation in payment systems.

Digital currencies allow for cross-border transactions to be completed more quickly, affordably, and securely than with traditional banking systems.

Instance: Through facilitating quicker and less expensive cross-border transactions, Ripple's XRP seeks to increase the effectiveness of international payments.

Result: Improved payment systems have the potential to increase trade efficiency, lower transaction costs, and streamline international trade.

Investing and Conjecturing:

Institutional and individual investors are drawn to cryptocurrencies as an asset class for speculation and investing. Increased market volatility and the creation of new financial products, such exchange-traded funds (ETFs) and Bitcoin futures, are the results of this. - **Instance**: The introduction of Bitcoin ETFs into a number of markets has given investors easier access to regulated cryptocurrency exposure. **Result**: Investing more in cryptocurrencies can spur innovation and market expansion, but there are risks associated with volatility and speculative bubbles.

Possible Difficulties and Possibilities

Regulatory Uncertainty (1): The legal landscape surrounding cryptocurrencies is constantly developing, and differing laws in different states might be confusing. Governments are battling over how to regulate digital assets in order to deal with problems pertaining to financial stability, consumer protection, and illegal activity. - Application: Stable environments for companies and investors can stimulate innovation and offer legal clarity when clear and uniform regulatory frameworks are in place. Difficulty: Uncertainty in the law and possible restrictions on particular businesses or resources may impede the expansion of the market and

innovation. **Privacy and Security Issues**: As the Bitcoin ecosystem expands, so do security and privacy concerns.
Users and platforms are exposed to serious dangers due to hacks, frauds, and vulnerabilities.

Opportunity:

New developments in privacy-enhancing and cybersecurity technology have the potential to increase the security and anonymity of bitcoin transactions.
Problem: Persistent security risks and privacy worries could damage user confidence and prevent widespread adoption.

Environmental Impact and Scalability:

For many blockchain networks, scalability is still an issue, especially when transaction volumes are large. Furthermore, because of their high energy consumption, some consensus processes, like Proof of Work, have sparked questions about their potential effects on the environment.

Opportunity: New developments in technology, including Proof of Stake and Layer 2 solutions, present an opportunity to address concerns related to scalability and the environment.

Problem: For cryptocurrencies and blockchain technology to be sustainable in the long run, scalability and environmental issues must be addressed.

Forecasts for the Upcoming Decade

Broad Acceptance: Increased use of cryptocurrencies is anticipated in a number of industries, including technology, retail, and banking.

The increasing maturity of infrastructure and legal frameworks may lead to a greater integration of cryptocurrencies into regular financial activities and services. - **Projection**: More companies and institutions will likely accept and use cryptocurrencies in their operations as digital currencies become the norm for payment.

Better Clarity on Regulations: We may anticipate more complete and lucid regulatory frameworks for cryptocurrencies throughout the course of the next ten years. More uniform regulations and rules pertaining to investor protection, financial stability, and market integrity will probably be established by governments and regulatory organizations.

<u>Projection</u>: Increased regulatory clarity will lessen confusion and possible legal concerns for users and businesses, while also stimulating innovation and institutional investment.

Technological Developments: Blockchain technology will spur the creation of new applications and enhance current ones. The bitcoin ecosystem's future will be shaped by innovations including scalability boosts, privacy advancements, and interoperability solutions.

<u>Projection</u>: The functionality, effectiveness, and user experience of cryptocurrencies will be improved by emerging technology, which will encourage wider adoption and new applications.

DeFi and Web3 Evolution:

It is anticipated that Web3 technology and the decentralized finance (DeFi) industry will develop further, bringing new financial services and decentralized applications that empower users and lessen dependency on conventional middlemen. **Projection**: Web3 and DeFi could revolutionize digital interaction, banking, and government in a number of ways, creating more decentralized and user-centric systems.

Combining Conventional Financial Systems with Integration: Cryptocurrencies will probably become more deeply integrated with established financial systems as they become more widely accepted. This may result in hybrid financial models that incorporate the best features of both traditional and digital banking. **Projection**: A more smooth financial ecosystem will be made possible by the emergence of collaboration models between traditional and cryptocurrency finance, as well as an increase in the number of services linked to cryptocurrencies that financial institutions offer. There is a lot of promise and uncertainty for cryptocurrencies in the future. Although developments like DeFi, blockchain interoperability, and the emergence of CBDCs indicate great progress, issues with security, scalability, and legislation still need to be resolved.

The course of cryptocurrencies in the upcoming ten years will be determined by advancements in technology, changes in regulations, and their incorporation into the world economy. Maintaining awareness and flexibility will be essential for surviving in this changing and dynamic environment.

www.ingramcontent.com/pod-product-compliance
Lightning Source LLC
Chambersburg PA
CBHW050310230526
45471CB00005B/2116